Allah and My Heart

Humera Malik
Illustrated by Basmah Syadza

Allah and My Heart:
Learning to Accept and Manage Our Big Feelings

Written by: Humera Malik
Illustrated by: Basmah Syadza

© Green Key Press 2022

All rights reserved. No part of this publication may be reproduced, stored in a retrieval system, or transmitted, in any form of by any means, without the prior permission in writing of Green Key Press, or as expressly permitted by law, license, or under terms agreed with the relevant reproduction rights organization. Inquiries concerning reproduction outside this scope should be sent to the publisher.

A publication of:
Green Key Press
Washington, DC

For further information, please visit greenkeypress.com.

ISBN 978-0-9989782-6-0
10 9 8 7 6 5 4 3 2 1

GREEN KEY PRESS

When someone has something I don't,
I feel jealous.

Allah says
He is never unfair
to anyone.

I can say,
'Allah make me grateful
for what You have given me,'

and I can count my blessings.

When it is dark outside, I feel scared.

I can say 'Allah is my protector,'

and read the last three surahs of the Quran.

When I have no one
to play with at lunch,
I feel lonely.

Allah says
He is my friend and
He is always with me.

I can say
'Allah is with me wherever I am,'
and I can do something
to make someone else feel special.

If someone I love goes to heaven,
I feel grief.

Allah says
with hard times come ease.

I can say 'everything belongs to Allah and everything returns to Allah,'

and I can cry to Allah.

If my sister wins the game,
I feel angry.

I can say
'I seek refuge in Allah,'
and I can stay quiet until
I feel calm again.

When I have too much to do,
I feel overwhelmed.

Allah says He does not give me
more than I can handle.

I can say
'Allah I am overcome, help me,'
and I can do dhikr to calm my body.

When I say something that upsets my friends, I feel guilty.

Allah says He is the most forgiving and loving.

I can say 'My Lord, forgive me,'

and I can say sorry.

If I have to talk in front
of the class,
I feel shy.

Allah says He is my helper.

I can say
'Allah, give me courage,'
And I can begin with Bismillah.

If I have a test at school,
I feel worried.

Allah says
put your trust in Me.

I can say 'Allah guide me,'

and leave my worries with Him.

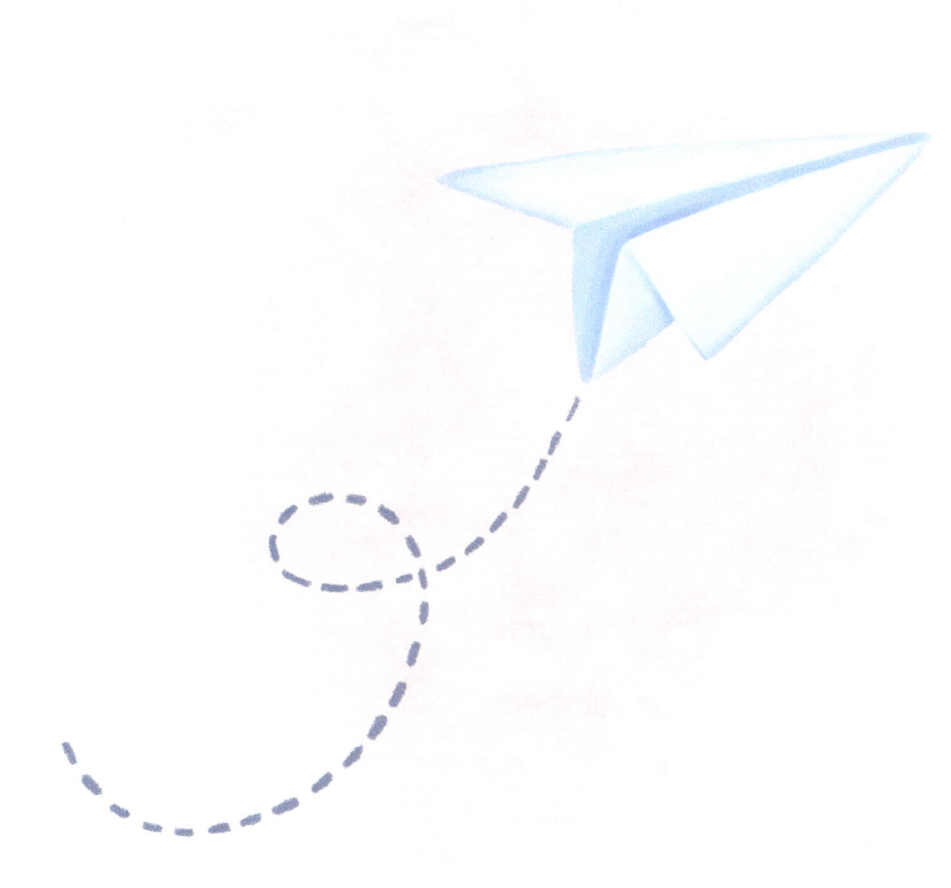

If I get to spend the day at the park,
I feel happy.

I can say
'All praise belongs to Allah,'

and offer an extra prayer.

Sometimes I don't know why,
but I just feel sad.

Allah says pray to Me,
I will answer your prayer.

I Can Say,

God

I am in need of anything good you send down to me

and I can talk to Allah.

www.ingramcontent.com/pod-product-compliance
Lightning Source LLC
Chambersburg PA
CBHW042130040426
42450CB00003B/137